Louis Daniel Brodsky's Holocaust-related poems are evocative, even hallucinatory; they belong to a time that is still drowning in oceans of ashes.

Elie Wiesel,
Nobel Peace Prize

In the opening poem of Louis Daniel Brodsky's *The Thorough Earth*, a salesman, Willy Sypher, hauls his cargo westerly. In the last poem, he prays that he will himself be cargo in a locomotive that will scream *past* Auschwitz and Dachau easterly toward God. Willy, a brooding presence in every poem here, is a peddler working from a cart in the old countries, and a contemporary member of the Chamber of Commerce who works out of his station wagon; he is a "fleer of pogroms" and at the same time an established citizen, is gregarious and bone-lonely, entrepreneur and "entremanure," garrulous and silent, demon of Teutonic children's dreams and harmless tailor-scapegoat, living poet and Auschwitz statistic (though he denies the latter, he knows the truth). Complex and obsessive with Willy's aspirations and fears, written because Brodsky has entered the ghetto with his ancestors and a grave new world of his own, this is a seamless and compelling book.

William Heyen,
author of *Erika: Poems of the Holocaust*

THE THOROUGH
EARTH

Books By
LOUIS DANIEL BRODSKY

Poetry

Trilogy: A Birth Cycle (1974)
Monday's Child (1975)
The Kingdom of Gewgaw (1976)
Point of Americas II (1976)
Preparing for Incarnations (1976)
La Preciosa (1977)
Stranded in the Land of Transients (1978)
The Uncelebrated Ceremony of Pants Factory Fatso (1978)
Birds in Passage (1980)
Résumé of a Scrapegoat (1980)
Mississippi Vistas (1983)
You Can't Go Back, Exactly (1988)
The Thorough Earth (1989)

Bibliography (Co-authored with Robert W. Hamblin)

Selections from the William Faulkner Collection of
    Louis Daniel Brodsky: A Descriptive Catalogue (1979)

Faulkner: A Comprehensive Guide to the Brodsky Collection:
    Volume I: The Biobibliography (1982)
    Volume II: The Letters (1984)
    Volume III: The De Gaulle Story (1984)
    Volume IV: Battle Cry (1985)
    Volume V: Manuscripts and Documents (1989)

Country Lawyer and Other Stories for the Screen by
    William Faulkner (1987)

Stallion Road: A Screenplay by William Faulkner (1989)

Biography

William Faulkner: Life Glimpses (1990)

THE THOROUGH EARTH

Poems by

Louis Daniel Brodsky

Louis Daniel Brodsky

12/20/07

St. Louis, MO.

Timeless Press
Saint Louis, Missouri

Timeless Press, Inc.
10411 Clayton Road
Saint Louis, Missouri 63131

Library of Congress Catalog Card Number: 89-50805

ISBN 1-877770-03-5
ISBN 1-877770-04-3 (pbk.)
ISBN 1-877770-05-1 (tape)
ISBN 1-877770-06-X (tape & pbk. set)

Designed by Ruth A. Dambach
Southeast Missouri State University
Manufactured in the United States of America

First Edition, First Printing (August 1989)

The author would like to express his gratitude to the editors of the following journals for permission to reprint poems first appearing in their pages:

The Southern Review. "Manager of Outlet Stores," "Young Willy Services Two Major Accounts," "A Day in the Life of Willy Sypher," "Résumé of a Scrapegoat," "Willy's Southern Route"

Pulpsmith. "Boxcars," "Panning for Gold"

Newsart. "Grandfather"

Ball State University *Forum.* "Cracow, Now!," "Emigré in the Promised Land," "Surviving Another Fall"

Harper's. "Death Comes to the Salesman"

Some of the poems in this volume appeared in different versions in the following previously published books by the author:

Point of Americas II (1976). "Panning for Gold"

Preparing for Incarnations (1976). "Grandfather"

Stranded in the Land of Transients (1978). "Manager of Outlet Stores," "Death Comes to the Salesman," "Willy"

Résumé of a Scrapegoat (1980). "Résumé of a Scrapegoat"

"Death Comes to the Salesman" was anthologized in *Voices from the Interior: Poets of Missouri* (1982, BkMk Press).

The following poems have been reprinted in annual editions of *Anthology of Magazine Verse and Yearbook of American Poetry*:

1981 Edition. "Death Comes to the Salesman"

1984 Edition. "A Day in the Life of Willy Sypher"

1985 Edition. "Willy's Southern Route"

1986-1988 Edition. "Young Willy Services Two Major Accounts"

1989 Edition. "Surviving Another Fall"

To Alan F. Pater, editor of the *Anthology of Magazine Verse* series, I extend my deepest thanks for the encouragement his selections of my work for his unique collections have given me.

I also wish to acknowledge my appreciation of Lewis P. Simpson, consulting editor of *The Southern Review*, whose respect for my traveling salesman poems, in particular, has been a fundamental source of inspiration for my poetry.

Editorially, Linda Hermelin has offered stylistic suggestions which I have gratefully incorporated into many of the poems in this collection.

Brodsky & Sons
Purveyors to the World

Daniel
1857 — 1926

   Louis Daniel (Lou)
   1885 — 1937

      Saul
      1909 —

         Louis Daniel (L.D.)
         1941 —

            Louis Daniel III (Troika)
            1977 —

May their line
always be
ahead of its Time

The whole chronicle of man's immortality is in the
suffering he has endured, his struggle toward the
stars in the stepping-stones of his expiations.
Intruder in the Dust — William Faulkner

CONTENTS

PEDDLER ON THE ROAD

THE ASHKEEPER'S EVERLASTING PASSION WEEK

PEDDLER
ON THE ROAD

Above all, the jeans needed a catchy label. "People want a name," says Eli Kaplan, the president of Englishtown Sportswear Ltd., which produces Sergio Valente jeans. Sergio Valente? He doesn't exist. "What's so bad?" says Kaplan. "Who was going to buy Eli Kaplan jeans?"

"The Jeaning of America" — *Newsweek*, 10/6/80

"I have nothing against jews as an individual," I says. "It's just the race. You'll admit that they produce nothing. They follow the pioneers into a new country and sell them clothes."

"You're thinking of Armenians," he says, "aren't you. A pioneer wouldn't have any use for new clothes."

"No offense," I says. "I don't hold a man's religion against him."

The Sound and the Fury — William Faulkner

Willy Sypher: A Poetics

Willy Sypher. Who is he? Foremost, he is a fictitious creation of the poet, imagined, but not imaginary, feigned, or ungenuine. He is not artificial or contrived in a literary sense, though he has had his origins in art and issues from a genealogy whose offspring are Song and Dance and Metaphor: a present-day ancient nomad and troubadour. For me, Willy Sypher is a "fiction" only in a strictly legal interpretation of the word. Indeed, he is an "assumption of a possible thing as a fact irrespective of the question of the truth." In Willy Sypher's existence, truth and fact blend with invention, obscure each other, lose their distinguishing features, finally rendering a composite portrait of a "real" man, a Jewish traveling salesman, seen from various perspectives in manifold dramatic situations throughout a career lasting more than half a century.

Born sometime around the end of the first decade of America's 20th century, entering the work force in the years just preceding the Great Depression, and reaching maturity as a successful sales representative for a large Midwestern men's clothing manufacturer during the forties and fifties, Willy Sypher came of age suffering few self-delusions or illusions about the nature of the "rag" business, the social worlds it "serviced," and his place and impact in relationship to both. Since taking to the road at age 18, he seemed to have possessed the ability to read his own ethnic code and to "decipher" its implications for himself. He recognized that his Jewishness relegated him to second-class status: he would never be accepted other than as a functionary, a human means to a materialistic end for shopkeepers, department store buyers, specialty store operators, even to associates in the "industry" requiring products, "goods" he could channel their way on a moment's notice. Not for a second did he believe that a smile was an all-day sucker or that a handshake served any purpose other than priming a pump, helping to grease a few palms.

Friendships, he realized early on, were fleet and at best tentative, no less susceptible to becoming threadbare than the trousers and suits and sports coats he sold daily, year in and year out. Essentially, Willy knew who he was, of what his identity consisted: his heritage, his purpose in the universe he canvassed, his fate and destiny. Nothing more, but nothing less! For all the cards he'd played with road cronies and countless hands of solitaire he'd endured in lonely motels, he never feared Death would deal him the two-eyed Jack of suicide.

If Willy Sypher's surname is redolent of etymologies signifying "nothing" or "empty" and if the definition often cited in dictionaries suggests "a person or thing of no importance or value; nonentity," Willy himself, in his optimistic thoughts and persistently opportunistic actions, defiantly disproves this formal epitaph; he belies the mathematical axiom that zero times anything is always zero or nothing. His existence does stand for something! It is a product, a force to be counted in that final number. And it is this tenacious faith in his ordinariness that accounts for his formidable resilience and fortitude in holding at bay rejection and bigotry and in circumventing natural roadblocks along highways his life's odyssey takes him.

As Willy's creator, I feel he has far less of me in him than I have him in me. He is much older than I; his experiences are fabled and filled with pervasive melancholy and oppression, as well as a passion for survival and at least a modicum of genuine compassion and humane wisdom, which in me have yet to be tested. Certainly, my untried attributes derive from plenty and comfort, legacies uniquely prevalent in America since the late-1940s. Curiously, my own self-willed immersion into the "rag" business was the impetus and origin of Willy Sypher's liberation from silence, as well as my own, and for his and my transcendence from the biblical aura of flown spirits who have lighted the way to the opening of my own day's cave. Perhaps Willy Sypher is the incarnation of 2000 years of living that at first I had tried to deny and to whose voices I had refused to give ear, failing to recognize they contained notes and measures of a poetry I would one day assimilate and transmute into my own.

As I see it now, Willy Sypher was one of the seminal agents and counterparts representing my heritage who had come to serve me with history's subpoena, a delivery boy issuing papers to my employer, Imagination, garnishing my wages until I might make good on some unstated obligation to my Conscience. And after all, maybe Willy had come to me hoping to justify the decency of *his* existence by selling me robes like those he'd once sewed and sold to Abraham and Moses, and thus justify my own!

Log-Thoughts South

At 6:00, I leave Oxford for West Helena
With cargo from the Holy Land
Where garments I haul in my wagon
Were sewn, pressed, and loaded
To be bartered for universal scrip
In factory outlet stores
I, a glorified delivery boy, oversee.

Ranging westerly toward Old Man,
Kudzu-smothered, red-clay hills
Give way to furrowed Delta.
Thank God the Hebraic strain
Shading my Yankee carpetbagger profile
Isn't as blatant to resident fates
As it seems to me, fleer of pogroms.

Ill at ease, I pass intact,
Arrive tired. My fears are "outlanderish!"
Yet, why tempt providence
Announcing my cut-rate presence
With newspaper ads and radio spots?
Inconspicuously, I make my stop,
Question bum checks, gaps in stock,

Bemoan profits, sky-rocketing utilities
As preludes to my Moses-Atop-Zion
Cross of Gold speech.
Rising to oratorical eloquence,
I beseech my salesclerks to squeeze blood
Out of each turnip plucked
From this Southern Garden of Eden.

After catfish buffet, we unpack my hold,
Reload it with "goods" too bad
To be sold, even by me,
Expert in "perfects," Merchant of Distress,
Purveyor to the Dispossessed,
Who's bargained with the Prince of Darkness
And never come out second best.

Then I drive off, jotting in my log
Thoughts my children might recite
To their kids decades hence
As reminders of their odd grandfather,
The road-peddler/poet,
Who, with three college degrees, ended up
Living out of his ancestors' tents.

Manager of Outlet Stores

He attends the Chamber of Commerce meeting
Once each month
For Monday lunch with merchants and professionals
And modestly regards himself
An integral part of the community's growth.

Although he leaves twice a week
In a station wagon weighted with goods
Being transferred from warehouse
To factory outlets in three states,
He considers Farmington his headquarters.

For all the alluring ladies
Loitering along sleazy hallways
Down which his bachelorhood leads,
The whore he best knows
And misses most passionately when home

Is the road that undresses his thoughts:
She fingers his rough spine with smooth hands,
Draws him into her soothing curves;
Coming and going, her fluid movements
Drive him crazy. Arriving is mindblowing.

The attachments he's made by chance
Extend to waitresses, leggy barmaids
He tips at night's climax with room keys,
Nightclerks taking wake-ups
And raspy complaints with bored restraint.

He smiles at their "Yes, sir... No, sir,
Right away, sir,"
Then places his "advanced reservation"
For "guaranteed late arrival," "ground floor,"
"Commercial rate" the following evening.

As itinerant minister of Surplus and Flaw,
Disciple of Not-Quite-Right merchandise,
Preaching providence, cheap prices,
And the gospel of impulse buying,
He reaches multitudes while touching few.

Young Willy Services Two Major Accounts

My Dear Mississippi Kiddo:

I regret my unannounced arrival in Jackson
Before heading on for New Orleans,
But business takes precedence,
Dictates schedule, destination, comportment:
Best foot forward, articulate wit,
Not raw passion, are de rigueur
If I'm to keep from risking my position
As mid-South rep
For Acme-Zenith Trouser of St. Louie, Mo.

Afraid of waking your husband,
I'm forced to leave this on your visor,
Escort that whore, Silence, to bed.
Dispossessed of your wet sex
And missing your touch and tongue
To reassure me the remote geography
I stumble into is safe,
I'll grope for morning's door,
Borrow tomorrow on this unsecured note.

Ah, but then, I see this abstinence
As discretionary compliance, token sacrifice
When measured against potential gains.
How otherwise might we sustain
The feverish pitch of our alliance?
Besides, cake consumed without savoring
Only tastes sweet to the baker.
Anyway, let's not belabor slack time —
I'll be back in forty-eight hours!

Mr. Willy

A Day in the Life of Willy Sypher

No Huckleberry Findelbaum am I,
But Willy Sypher,
Peddler to the Midwestern territory
Serviced by Acme-Zenith Clothing,
Lighting out again this lonely morning,
Not even hoping to open new accounts,
Just hold my own
Against competition and a limp economy.

The road has come to own me,
Dreams and soul, body, spirit, volition
(Synonyms line up at my heart's gate
To gain audience with my popish tongue).
I've known so many homes
These past twenty-five centuries:
Bedouin tents, nomadic oases, posadas,
Hostels, motels, boarding houses.

Gas station attendants, reservationists,
Waitresses, union musicians,
Bartenders are the ephemerae
In my unchanging equation for transience.
Uprootedness is crucial to erosion;
The topsoil in the cradle
Through which I commute is constantly removed,
Replaced by newer sediments.

Yet, I alone remain untouched
By each upheaval
As I hustle overstocks and "thirds,"
Garments not-quite-perfect
For mill flaws, manufacturing defects,
And hawk merchandise from swatch books,
Samples locked in my trunk,
Pushing worsteds and corduroy in July,

Cotton tropicals and whisper flannels in February.
Unphased by such paradoxes,
I've grown accustomed to existence
Lived upside-down, inside-out.
Despite marrying a Midianite wife
Who raised two kids in my hiatus,
My entire life
Has been a night shift bereft of family ties.

Just now, I press westward,
Hurrying to arrive in time for lunch
With the buyer for Quicksilver's in Tipton,
A mama and papa shop
I've called on for thirty-five years.
As I approach and park,
Signs splayed on the plate glass curse me:
GONE OUT OF BUSINESS — PERMANENTLY!

Willy in His Prime

Just the act of exiting the City
Against traffic's surge and lurch
Is sufficient consolation to make work
No mere matter of road travel,
But holy Crusade in the service of Kings.

Although no one ever promised Moses
Nomadic existence would lead to an oasis
Or Quixote would save Dulcinea
From his broom-closet hallucinations,
Plying the highways by myself

Lets me exercise blind faith in freedom.
Eluding Levites, Ethiopes,
Televangelists praying in theme parks
Along royal trade routes,
I excel showing my line to loyal clientele.

Take today! On an April this zippy,
Even if ordered to drive my own hearse,
I doubt I'd alter this trip an iota
Just to arrive on time. Face it,
I've got accounts you just don't keep waiting!

Willy

Myriad, yet so immutable,
Are the mind's stopping-off places
He chooses to occupy nightly
On gloomy trips away from acquaintances,
He doesn't even know when he's gone.

Loitering in dim-lit motel crypts
Separating the outside air
From an even emptier indoors,
He personifies wandering Moses;
His fleshy pores are eddies of sweat.

Wiping the bathroom mirror
To clear it of his invisible tears,
He smudges the glass, escapes recognition
By eyes peering through eyes
Hiding behind his one-way brain.

When fatigue comes near,
He resists circumventing desperation
By refusing to take capsules and tablets,
Enters no-man's-land alone.
He's crossed entire Saharas on his knees!

Sleeping beneath sleazy sheets
Inside his forsaken bag of being,
Without even the solace of a female body,
Evokes monastic stoicism
That almost glorifies his loneliness.

Each dawn is his apotheosis.
He blends into clothing, sifts the dark
For an opening, then sets out prophetically
With swatch cards and sample garments
To service the bargain basements of his heart.

Willy's Southern Route

Scalawag, rapscallion, abolitionist,
Ragman carpetbagger:
Apposite nicknames; I've been called them all
Time and again with vicious derisiveness
And outspoken indignation on trips to Mississippi,

And worse. "Nigger-lovin' Jew,
Who needs your kind here in Jefferson?"
Mr. Compson yelled last week
From his hardware store porch on the Square
As I approached Klein's Dry Goods.

Whether it's the two gold caps,
Nose not-quite-patrician for its hook
Just below the bridge, vested suit
Even in July's booking season,
Or ACME-ZENITH — ST. LOUIS stenciled on my cases,

I can't say with certainty.
Regardless, their eyes, like rusted scythes,
Slice a raspy path across my shadow
Walking sidewalks, crossing streets behind me
With shrill obscenities and threats;

Spit just misses hitting me
As I pass their somnolent buzzard-huddled bodies
Squatting on splintered benches
About the Courthouse. In abject silence
My outraged class-consciousness dis-integrates.

Neither Moses nor the Nazarene among zealots,
But Willy Sypher, Midwest sales rep,
I schlep seconds and overstocks
Slightly out of my element,
Trying to make a killing without being crucified,

Hoping to buy time selling on time
Despite inimical racial and religious odds.
Thank God for small favors!
All my competitors, whether based in New Orleans
Or Breman, Georgia, are also second class.

God only knows, there's got to be room
In the magnolia, mockingbird, and toddy code
For a few Jews; even Ku Kluxers
Have to wear trousers and suits. Who knows,
Their robes probably come from Klein's, too!

Willy: Fisher of Men

I set out from my Jefferson City motel
Heading home this soiled a.m.,
Gnawed to the bone by store buyers
And their "go-fers" like a pig's carcass
Thrown into the Amazon;

Heading home via Holts Summit,
New Bloomfield, Fulton,
Finally arriving at Kingdom City
(A far cry from Paradise or earthly Canaan!)
Where I bisect highway 70;

Heading home with my week's meager catch
Of net-thirty, "bone-a-Fido" orders.
(Damn! Feeding out next April's line
An entire July in advance
Is like trying to catch man-eaters by hand!);

Heading home to my apartment at Waterman
And Delmar, its halls reeking ghetto recipes:
Eternally simmering gefilte fish,
Matzo ball broth, chicken necks.
I bite my lip, savor its Seder taste

As if the Red Sea had never parted,
And remember that, though neither poet
Nor upside-down Jascha Heifetz,
I'm no Auschwitz statistic
Or bone-smoulder seething over Poland, either,

But rather Acme-Zenith's Midwest rep,
The *best* and *only* for forty years,
Who yet can sell hell out of a suit
Missing its sleeves and lapels,
Slacks lacking zipper and back pockets,

And who, at 60, still can swallow whole,
Easy as egg in my beer,
Piranha and Jewfish alike!
All I request is, when convenient,
Serve them kosher, preferably filleted!

Death Comes to the Salesman

It happened so fast,
The sun slipping past the black gates
Into this hoary morning,
I felt compelled to frisk the mist
Lifting from roadside hills and valleys
To allay my anxiety that sunlight,
Not the ochreous body of death,
Had thrown its shadows
Over my future with so little notice.

Yet, when I sent out my eyes
To scrutinize its vapors, they were gone,
And in their place, everywhere,
Vision was a painfully blinding haze
Clawing across a tender sky.
In defense, I drew the visor down,
Limiting sight to the pavement on fire,
A bubbling River Styx,
Until I was no longer the driver,

But a victim drowning
In midstream in a netherworld,
Ferried to the earth's furnace.
By the time I finally arrived for my meeting,
I'd completely forgotten the reason
For leaving home so early, or even
In whose body I'd slept last evening
Before dying with such abruptness
On this perfectly normal Saturday morning.

The Loneliness of an Old Road Peddler

These days, Willy spends his retirement
Suspended in contemplation of friends
Upon whom he depends to keep memory
From surrendering to sedentariness,
Succumbing to forgetfulness, dementia,
Descending into that endless cave
Whose myriad mazy chambers are the punishment
Old age imposes on sinners and innocents
With arbitrary arrogance and temerity.

Yet, curiously, it's been almost a decade
Since he last spoke with anyone at Acme-Zenith
Or jotted a note of condolence,
Mailed greeting cards at Christmas and Easter
To loyal gentile clientele
And good-old-boy goyem he'd met
In motels and local cafés fifty years wide,
Five states deep,
Oases in the Midwest desert he'd plied.

At least ten years have elapsed
Since Willy last sent Chanukah gifts
To members of his congregation, the boss's son,
His deceased wife Leah's nephews and nieces,
Said his shaloms, l'chaims, mazel tovs
At Passover, Yom Kippur, Rosh Hashanah,
Brises, bar mitzvahs, and weddings
Of brothers and sisters of the Tribe
Wearing invisible frontlets between their eyes.

But all too often these days
His friends seem to rise like sweat beads
Through pores in persecutorial dreams,
Not as faces from his salad days,
But gawking, hawk-nosed ragmen and grocers
Vending rotten Jewfish, moldy matzos,
Or scrofulous prophets stooping in soup lines,
And frail tailors stitching body bags
For victims of usurers and mail-order lawyers.

And in his loneliest moments,
While waiting for tomorrow's paper to be thrown,
Listening to traffic's slapstick below,
Or startled by garish nightmares
Shooting to the surface of fluorescent pools
He dove into viewing test patterns,
Willy knows who'll show up at his funeral
To hear the rabbi's graveside eulogy:
Just Death, his sole next of kin!

THE ASHKEEPER'S
EVERLASTING PASSION
WEEK

The tumult and the shouting dies;
  The captains and the kings depart:
Still stands Thine ancient sacrifice,
  An humble and a contrite heart.
Lord God of Hosts, be with us yet,
Lest we forget — lest we forget!
              "Recessional" — Rudyard Kipling

And the Lord said unto Cain: "Where is Abel thy
brother?" And he said: "I know not; am I my
brother's keeper?"
                                    Genesis 4.9

Grandfather

For Uncle Sam and Aunt Ann Brodsky

Damn it . . . God, damn it,
    that dear man is dying of cancer:
He refuses to eat or be fed intravenously,
Desires to die in bed at home, desires
To die,
    and here I am lamenting his loss
As though I know him for the close friend
I wish he had become,
    rather than the shadow
Of a vague acquaintanceship we'd made
On occasional High Holidays and Friday nights.
    We're the keepers of their ashes,
        those gone souls
Devastated by wars among their leaders,
People marked by signposts on their lintels
And frontlets between their frightened eyes
    to be spared Pharaohs' famines and blights
For the cyanide.
    We're their keepers
In spirit, self-appointed, properly anointed
With a seminal heritage we share
    through ancient marriages.
Our births, though 55 years apart,
Are marked by a tribal family name
Sealed in common ceremony.
    That dying man,
With whom only once I tried to reason
Concerning the meaning of a living religion,
Is reason enough for my lamentation:
His loss is mine;
    his departing shadow
Will deprive me of that constant reminder
That all those gone people
    rely on Me
To substantiate the decency of their existence.

Cracow, Now!

For Darlene Mathis-Eddy

Defeated, exiled, indefensibly committed,
Those dispensable souls
Relegated to the ghetto in Cracow!
Bankers, Talmudic scholars, grocers, musicians,
Strict, disciplined family men
Whose reverential Leahs, Rachels, Miriams
Bore in pride brilliant children!
Ghosts now, still guiding wheelbarrows
Filled with pillows and sheets
From cultured salons in family estates
To ventilator shafts, attics,
And dead air space between rooms
In hovels cluttering memory's tear ducts.

The metamorphosis of three centuries
Accomplished in months: Jew-Lice-Typhus!
Then the Madagascar Plan!
In the end, only Hitler's witless tactics —
Matching his storm troopers
Against Russia's forces of winter —
Could suspend the Final Solution
For tribes confined to greenhouses
Producing a variety of Venus' flytraps
So profuse neither Linnaeus
Now Darwin could have classified them:
Auschwitz, Treblinka, Belzec,
Dachau, Bergen-Belsen, Birkenau!

Just writing these bleak syllables chokes me!
Each is a puff of black smoke
Escaping crematoria stacks
Punctuating skylines of my verse,

***

Each a caesura too frequently breathed.
This morning, four decades downwind,
The measures of my sanity dwindle.
I, too, as messenger for the Dispossessed,
Wearing a "J" on my brain-band,
Push all my earthly belongings, paltry words,
In a rickety wheelbarrow across the years
Toward precarious lodging
In the ghettos of *your* unsuspecting ears.

Ossuary

Outside, the falling snow is frozen rain
Slowed to the pace of souls
Tracing their echoes home through space.

It no longer smells wet or glistens
As a month ago it did;
Instead, it partakes of momentary shapes

I suspicion could consist of ghostdust
Sifting down to earth
From pulverized spirits emitting odors

Foreboding and redolent of present-day
Bergen-Belsen and Sobibor.
A necromancer's spell suspending the land

In feckless slow-motion compels me
To question my location,
Motives for living, old notions of dying.

Suddenly, an image of Death shaving bones
Into scrimshaw slivers
To give as gifts to mistresses and pimps

Sends shivers to the ends of my vertebrae.
I cringe at the possibility
This impinging snow could be Me,

My atoms flaking off an imagination
Daring to provoke such
Grotesqueries by probing the "Verboten."

Ghetto Echoes

Sourceless screeching phonemes and moaning
Rise above this floating island
Dividing older, flown voices
From the present strophes of my groping verse;
Their measures cast backward glances
As they trudge line by line
Like clubfeet indenting trenches,
Not prints, in a sandy beach
Bordered by a roaring crematorium
Spitting obituaries into their disappearing tracks.

I listen for specific rhythmic signatures
And verbal idiosyncracies
Which might let me differentiate murmurs
Of tribe members, who never reached me alive,
From imaginary groaning
Generated from furnaces burning at the center
Of Memory's death camps.
But no identifiable inflections
Or ethnic dialects inscribe my inner ears
With familial threnodies.

Instead, a salt-sea silence
Inundates my verse, then evaporates,
Leaving behind it a stench-ridden shore
Pitted with calcified bones.
Suddenly alone,
Racing hysterically toward safe closure
With only fragments of this poem
To fix my soul's dislocation,
I recognize those moans as my own,
Trying to escape my throat's Lodz ghetto.

One Out of Six Million

At what point he entered the Void,
Became the point,
Eviscerated all antecedent penetrations,
Refuses public scrutiny,
Loses itself in diffusive philo-syllogisms.

His invisibility this too sunny morning
Is nowhere more apparent
Than in the words he tries to set free
To bribe immortality with diamonds,
Hide-and-seek victims bound for Gröss-Rosen

His mind's Cracovian Aktions expose
In word-scourges imposed on his ghettoed dignity.
His deloused poems huddle nakedly,
Awaiting Ukranian razors
To shave their pubic hair and armpits,

Render them fit for pyres and crematoria
From whose fetid stench
No phoenixes shall rise or survivors' cries
Be recycled into rhyme-lives;
Ah, but not until they've defied Time

One lacerating syllable after another,
Albeit with stuttering mutters
From articulating Xyklon-B showers;
Not until their verses are buried alive
In mass chasms fluting the air like salt domes.

He stares directly into the homicidal sun;
In a last lucid flash,
His flesh and bones, blistered, blasted, atomized,
Pass back through the Void,
Rejoin Youth's jubilant, cultivated voices

As though no shtetl, ghetto,
Or Holocaust ever erupted from daymares.
Suddenly he sees himself atop Mt. Zion
On his knees, piecing together the shattered tablets,
Reciting his own stone-poems to the Philistines.

Black Hole-O-Caust

> There are evils so deep you can
> drop names in them and never hear
> them hit bottom. Josef Mengele is
> one of those names.
>
> Stefan Kanfer — *People*

Voices squirm in his tongue's loose grip,
Mindlessly trying to wriggle free
Before being gyved to a final solution,
Tossed into a sea of obsolete clichés
Swarming with frenzied religions and creeds
Strafing greenish fathoms
For baited breaths: he con-trolls
Who decides for which species he'll fish.

A few elude articulation's barb,
Slide back into silence,
Avoid bloating, being swallowed alive
By appetites cruising for opportunities
To improve efficiency meeting quotas
And devise superior means
For eliminating entire schools of thought
In a solitary bite.

The rest get sacrificed collectively
To fiery trial by water.
Plunged into the Xyklon alembic
In which all false hopes are refined,
They disappear. No echoes resurface,
Just fumy spume rises.
Whatever secrets they may have possessed
Keep sifting deeper into the depths.

Résumé of a Scrapegoat

Every highway I drive,
With sideboards straining to contain goods
Brought up out of steerage,
Is Hester Street,

And I'm the displaced waif
A hundred ancient Diasporas left behind
To hawk rags and stitched shit
Made in sweaty lofts and dank basements.

I'm the entremanure of flawed raiments,
Remainders dead as flounder
Stacked flat on shelves
Or hanging in static masses from racks,

The lowest-class capitalist
Searching low and lower for newer Laputas
In whose depraved precincts
I might display my thieves' market.

I'm the wide-smiling, gold-filled mouth,
The glistening, beady eye,
The hook-nosed, seven-foot shadow
That demonizes Teutonic children's dreams,

The eternal, stereotypical victim
Hanging by my three pawned balls
Above the shattered plate glass Emporium
Cluttered with xenophobic bigotries.

I'm the scrapegoat for last season's guilt,
Soiled hopes, dreams with tiny holes,
Spirits returned for overlooked defects,
Mismatched leisure lifestyles,

The robber baron impeding competition
By fixing prices on perfects
I label "Irregular" and flawed garments
I advertise as "Grade A" merchandise.

History's kiss has touched my lips
With the viper's flicking tongue,
Singled me out from the crowd
To toil in dirty street curbs and alleys

With cunning and guile, quietly,
By the sweat of my Semitic brow,
Crawling nakedly on my scaly belly
To avoid being swastikaed by sign crews

Gluing posters on every available board
With news of another outlet store
Or wholesale chain opening
In a strip mall or shopping center, Amen!

Shit! I'd give my eyetooth
Just to be the solid gold watch
Tucked neatly in Pierpont Morgan's
Well-stretched Protestant vest pocket

Instead of a thimble-fingered tailor
Drawing chalk lines and pinning seams
Across the whim of every fat ass
Able to afford his own graded patterns.

Yet, History's also nourished me
With fruits from the tree of life eternal;
I've peddled myself from one generation
To the next, a perpetual hand-me-down,

Promoting my own brand of survival
At cut-rate prices, offering my soul,
On a moment's notice, to anyone
Who'd wear robes like those I sewed for Moses.

Emigré in the Promised Land

Warsaw looms cold and ghetto-gaunt
As King David's first temple
Gone to ash and dust
Whenever I sniff memories
Sifting into History's nostrils.

Odors my soul inhales
Are not Proustian teacakes,
But stale bread loaves
Smuggled through holes in *SS* nets,
Rotting bones, rat droppings, plagues.

Images of naked women and men,
Screwed to crematoria gates,
Shower doors, and oven lids
As human hinges on Death's portals,
Ulcerate my stomach linings,

And I puke blood instead of saliva.
I wish I knew why my intellect
Hasn't been able to remove its tatoo,
Erase the "J"
From its identification papers,

Or, without losing bowel control,
Accept Fate's scapegoating the Jew,
Castrating his testicles,
Injecting her breasts with estrogen
To fatten them for Nazi butcher shops.

Sometimes, quite late at night,
I hear them chanting, "Juden! Juden!"
And fear dreams will make me strip,
Then shoot and bootheel me
Into a pit of writhing swastikas

From which waking will be no escape,
Just perpetuation of daily life
Here in Israel. Hitler's vision fulfilled!
Maybe Madagascar
Would have been Canaan after all!

Panning for Gold

In among the ash heaps
Prospectors haggle over the gold teeth;
Each keeps a daily assay record
Of nuggets he retrieves: caps and inlays
Once securely positioned
In upper-class European circles
Of smartly dressed patronesses of the arts,
Sophisticated financiers, politicians,
Concert pianists, and rabbis
Named Jacobs, Weinstein, Prinzmetal,
Schwartzkopf, Kalish, Abrams,
Rabinovitz, and Glazer.
Now, forty-three years later,
Bounty hunters shake their sieves
At Buchenwald, Auschwitz, Dachau:
Their death rattles shatter the silence
With white noise so loud
It would wake the dead were any still alive.

As the teeth are brought to auction,
Bidders grow restless; they get frenzied,
Aggressive, hostile, genocidal;
Their ear-to-ear sneers
Expose myriad gold-filled cavities,
Intricate bridges and plates.
Dealers trip over numb tongues,
Bite lips to bleeding,
Quixotically jumping their own bids
To insure sufficient commissions.
After all, they have clients worldwide
Whose collections are complete,
Except for the extremely precious teeth.

The Thorough Earth

He moves ahead by fits,
Suffers amnesiac fugues and hallucinations
Every few days or weeks,
Stutters, halts, fidgets unpredictably
Like needles of an E.K.G. machine
Whenever he hears sirens
Or sees police; they arrest his thoughts,
Hurl him back to that Nazi Hell
Before he'd fled Berlin for Argentina,
Then to St. Louis, Missouri, his Elba.

Although more than forty years
Have worn away the most horrific details
Of gargoyled paranoia
That surmounted and drained his spirit's temple
In those ghettoed seasons
After that latter-day Wagner
Perforated the world's eardrums
With his demoniac baton,
He still sees in his mirrored eyes
Fear's shattered stained glass windows,

Still realizes that beneath the smooth facade
His low-profiled anonymity projects,
The old trepidation festers.
Today he appears inordinately upset.
Whether it's graffiti recently splattered
On Sleep's side streets and alleys,
Cops surrounding a shot President
Pervading his TV screen,
Or swastikas taped to his shop windows,
He can't say with certainty.

Maybe it's the dust of Kristallnacht
Or just the sheer weight of years
Crushing his skull to dull pain,
Exploding his brains, quashing his spirit.
Abruptly he collapses before his store;

***

Blood gushes from his nostrils;
His vested suit, pressed dress shirt
Serve as makeshift shrouds
During the hour's hiatus
Before strangers identify his corpse.

Another forty-five minutes elapse
As police, city coroner, and ambulance
Conclude their routine removal of evidence
Suggesting Death ever arrived and left.
Before going, they padlock the door,
Place cards vaguely resembling "J's"
In his darkened display windows,
And outline in yellow chalk
The Star of David shape of his crumpled body
On the sanitized sidewalk.

Now silence descends;
Twilight shadows efface from his store sign
All traces of *Estate Diamonds,*
Leaving intact only his last name's
First half: *Lieber*mann.
Briefly relieved, the empty street sighs
While fastidious Earth,
Elated over having satisfied her belated claims
On an unapprehended enemy,
Renews her search for the unexterminated.

Chelmno Rain

God gave Noah the rainbow sign;
No more water, the fire next time.

No rainbows redeem morning's storm,
Whose jagged blitzkriegs
Across the sky oozing cyanic to purple
Might be the hues of brilliance at synapse
Or universe collapsing back on itself
Through a massive black hole.
No matter, my nerves don't desert me
In loneliness' no-man's-land.

Although I keep my vehicle clean,
Traces of feces and urine-stained straw
Stick to seat covers and roof liner
Like dog hairs or lice.
Older destinies conspire with water,
Fire the moaning tires
To Wagnerian caterwauling.
My station wagon heads Fate's cortège.

Driving home, I sense impending arrival
At any of ten thousand Chelmnos
Outlining my route.
But dying alone or amidst six million
Makes little difference to me.
I've always believed living by the Covenant,
For the Chosen anyway, means freedom
To choose my own rainbow!

Surviving Another Fall

Standing by innocently
This inordinately warm November morning,
Ankle-deep amidst shriveled leaves
Resembling molted locust husks
Or tiny clenched fists grasping at my shoes,
I listen to whispering benedictions
As each drifts down,
Brushes against kindred spirits,
Touches ground, and comes to rest
In a collective contritional gesture
Reminiscent of Auschwitz stick figures
Crammed into human strip mines.

Stricken by a vague, untraceable terror,
My shivering bones refuse to move.
Paranoia betrays vision.
Suddenly, swastikas litter the yard;
Nazi graffiti bloody my corneas;
Each leaf is a Gestapo agent
Informing storm troopers of my Jewishness.
Then they're leaves again, just leaves!
As their carrion odor dissipates,
For a moment I *almost* believe
This is nature's season, not another atrocity
Intended to defoliate a whole family tree.

Boxcars

Let me die inside a cattle car
Rattling behind a steam locomotive
Screaming past Auschwitz and Dachau,
Easterly toward God!
Let my dying be recorded on its sides:
Toxic, Flammable, Radioactive,
That even in demise
My life shall be considered volatile,
Heeded with *Extreme Caution!*
Let death highball me
Through seizing red semaphores
Between here and Eternity's golden depot,
As though I were precious cargo
Worthy of a Pullman suite,
Not a hobo's trackside sleep
By a remote Jewverville!
Let me go headlong over the Abyss
In rolling stock with hotboxes sparking
So that Charon's darkness
Will flicker hysterically with my passing!
Let me die happy
Inside a boxcar bound for Paradise!

LOUIS DANIEL BRODSKY

Louis Daniel Brodsky was born in St. Louis, Missouri, in 1941, where he attended St. Louis Country Day School. After earning a B.A., Magna Cum Laude, at Yale University in 1963, he received an M.A. in English from Washington University in 1967 and an M.A. in Creative Writing from San Francisco State University in 1968.

Mr. Brodsky is the author of fourteen volumes of poetry as well as nine scholarly books on Nobel laureate William Faulkner. Listing his occupation as Poet, he is also an adjunct instructor at Mineral Area College in Flat River, Missouri, Curator of the Brodsky Faulkner Collection at Southeast Missouri State University in Cape Girardeau, Missouri, and President of Timeless Press, Inc., St. Louis.

With his wife Jan, daughter Trilogy, and son Troika, he lives in St. Louis, Missouri.